AF540918

BIRD BUSINESS

What do you see when you watch a bird?

There is plumage to admire, identification marks to look out for, and song to lose oneself in. But beyond all this is their behaviour – the stealth of the hunter, the charisma of a male out to woo his mate and the sheer exuberance of flight. All of this explodes in brilliant colour and detail in the illustrations that light up this book. Rohan uniquely weaves together art and science with his trademark humour to give you a ringside seat to the daily dramas that make up the lives of birds. This is a book that goes beyond field guides and documentaries to help you see birds as never before.

India has a fantastic diversity of birds, all unique from one another in riveting ways. This book describes the antics of about a hundred. Flip over, read, revel!

BIRD BUSINESS

Dive into the fascinating lives of Indian birds

Rohan Chakravarty

JUGGERNAUT BOOKS
C-I-128, First Floor, Sangam Vihar, Near Holi Chowk,
New Delhi 110080, India

First published by BNHS 2019
Published by Juggernaut Books 2025

10 9 8 7 6 5 4 3 2 1

P-ISBN: 9789353459673
E-ISBN: 9789353453725

Layout and Design in Myriad Variable Concept by R. Ajith Kumar, Noida

Printed at Thomson Press India Ltd

Image captions for –
Front cover: Blue-Tailed Bee-Eater
Back cover: Asian Green Bee-Eaters
Page i: Asian Green Bee-eater, Indian Paradise-Flycatcher, Pied Kingfisher, Gould's Sunbird
Page iii: White-throated Kingfisher
Page iv: Ibisbill
Page v: Common Tailorbird nest
Page vii: Grey Peacock-Pheasants
Page 109: Dabbling duck: Indian Spot-billed Duck
Page 110: Great Crested Tern (left) and Arctic Jaeger (right)
Page 111: Indian Scops-Owl

In memory of my mother, Sulabha Chakravarty

Contents

Foreword

Art and science come together rarely; they come together with humour even more rarely. In this book, as in much of Rohan Chakravarty's work, they all meld beautifully, with touches of allure, sensitivity and grace. Here, he brings to life in his unique style the lifestyle quirks and natural history of a hundred-odd species of Indian birds. Each artful page on a particular species grabs you with its visual and aesthetic appeal. It also distils information on the bird's habits and natural history, and bustles with the vitality, peculiarity and idiosyncrasies of that bird's behaviour. And all of this is done in a manner that no field guide, bird book, encyclopaedia or video documentary on Indian birds has ever achieved.

This is a chirpy and sprightly book, brimming with life, with scarcely a dull moment in its pages. The birds leap and glide and whistle and wag and swoop and spear and court and cavort. They dive into oceans and wing over mountains, they chisel into trees and probe into mud, they sing their hearts out and serenade their mates, they nest in trees and houses and earth-tunnels and mounds, they gobble garbage and slurp nectar, they drink and dance and do the doo-doo. There's so much liveliness in each page and the behaviour of each species is illustrated so well that you may be tempted to flip quickly to the next page, skipping past the words to the next eye-catching illustration. But that would be a mistake. The writing, too, is not to be missed. Rohan's brief word-portraits of the birds, and accurate and charming descriptions of their curious adaptations and behaviours will bring you many a chuckle, much jaw-dropping astonishment and ultimately, a new or renewed intimacy with these wonderful birds.

For children and adults, there is much to learn within these pages. I say this not just as an admirer of Rohan's work, but as a hobby birdwatcher for over thirty-five years and a bird researcher for at least half that period. I learnt much that I never knew and experienced a renewed delight in the little that I did, seeing it portrayed in such a unique way. The species illustrated here also offer a glimpse of India's remarkable diversity of 1,300 bird species: from the very familiar House Sparrow and Barn Swallow, the Black Kites of our cities, the Cattle Egrets of our countryside and the daytime larks and eagles to the nightjars and owls, and rarities like the Satyr Tragopan and the endangered Great Indian Bustard.

The book both reveals and evokes a love for birds and a concern over their plights and lives. In our rapidly changing planet, the plight of birds only reflects our own plight and, in that sense, bird business is our business too. This you can discover for yourself when you turn to the delightful pages that follow.

T.R. Shankar Raman
Ecologist and Author

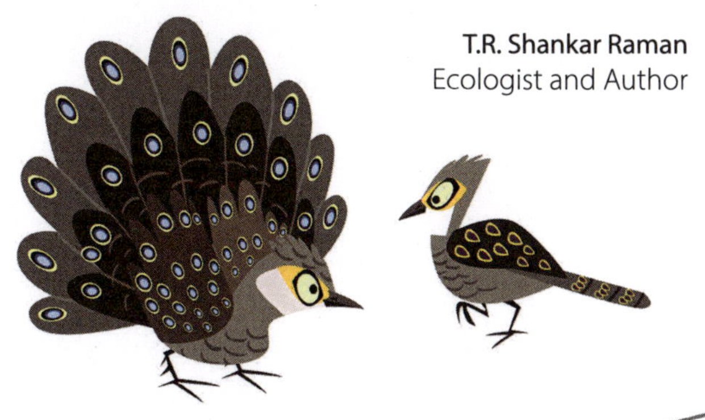

Introduction

'What is a bird?' Everyone has an answer to that question. 'Which is your favourite bird?' We all have a favourite bird by now, I'm sure. 'What does your favourite bird do all day?' Now that is a tricky one. Field guides seldom address this question. Encyclopaedias do, but leave most of the visuals to our imagination. Ornithologists know the answer, but they are busy dissecting owl pellets most of the time.

Bird Business offers a glimpse into the daily lives of birds from the Indian subcontinent through illustrations. Illustrated sequences take you through the specialities of each species and its role in nature. The book is more a celebration of the diversity in bird behaviour rather than that of bird species. I hope that the book will enable the birdwatcher to appreciate the romance of watching birds better, and entice the uninitiated into the vivid avian world. India has close to 1,300 species of birds, all unique from one another in riveting ways. This book describes the antics of about a hundred. Flip over, read, revel!

An Asian Green Bee-eater hunts

Although it is called a 'bee-eater', every insect that can be caught on the wing is fair game for the bird. Open ends of tree branches are its preferred perch, from where it frequently scans the skies for winged tidbits. Its long tail and the wire-like extensions make it an extreme aerial acrobat, and the sharp twists and turns it makes in pursuit of its prey can put veteran fighter pilots to shame. Once caught, the bee-eater returns with the insect to its favourite perch but isn't quite done with dinner preparations yet. It whacks its catch repeatedly on the perch in order to immobilize it and disable the sting. It then tosses up its meal with the flair of a pizza chef and gulps it down in a blink.

In the breeding season, the bee-eater courts his mate by chivalrously offering freshly caught insects to impress her. 

An Osprey preys

You might think that this is just another 'fish-eating raptor next door'. But look carefully and you'll notice that the Osprey stands out. Ospreys have a hunting technique unique among raptors. The large bird's eyesight is so well-developed that it can see clearly beneath the surface of the water. When it spots a fish, it hovers, momentarily, mid-air, to lock its target and swoops down at tremendous speed, almost surrendering to gravity. It stretches its feet out in line with the head, so as to maximize aerodynamics, and plunges into the water headfirst, often submerging itself. Moments later, the Osprey makes a graceful reappearance above the water with the quarry clutched parallel to its body with its opposable talons (again, a unique feature that enables a tight grip even in flight), and heads to a safe perch to devour it.

An Indian Paradise-Flycatcher goes flycatching

If Indian birds participated in a beauty pageant, the Paradise Flycatcher could well be the showstopper of the night. Its elaborate caudal ornaments place it right next to the Birds of Paradise on the 'glamour-meter'. A hunter on the wing, that looks for food in the understorey, it launches itself at the sight of a flying insect. It may seem like the excessively long tail could complicate matters for the bird, but it only adds to the grace of the act. The bird moves about like a fairy in the thick vegetation, its plumage contrasting sharply with the green of its habitat. Once caught, the prey is taken to the cozy, cup-shaped nest built carefully at the fork of a tree, and fed to an ever-hungry chick.

A Pied Kingfisher goes fishing

Boldly coloured in black and white, the Pied Kingfisher watches over a clear lake from its favourite stump perch. Its large eyes pierce the water surface, making the underwater menu for the day visible to this eagle-eyed hunter. When the selection is made, the kingfisher starts to hover mid-air, its eyes fixed on its target, while the rest of its body moves in fluttering motion. Suddenly, the bird drops down like a bullet, penetrating the water surface with a splash. Two fractions of a second later, when the bird emerges with a glistening fish in its long bill, you often find yourself clapping in amazement!

An Asian Openbill's unique 'tableware'

A visit to just about any Indian wetland will acquaint you with an odd-looking stork. The gap in its bill is so awkward that you cannot help but wonder how it contributes to the stork's life. But this unique adaptation is actually precision-cutlery. The Openbill's favourite food, giant apple snails, have huge, tough and sturdy shells encasing their soft bodies. While most snail-eaters would first have to worry about cracking the shell open, the Openbill simply slides the tip of its lower bill into the snail's case, prodding its body out without much damage to the shell itself! A bizarre gastronomical adaptation to feast on gastropods!

A Bengal Florican courts

'Love is always a leap into the unknown,' writes romance novelist Lisa Kleypas. For the Bengal Florican, leaping into the air is a way of grabbing his prospective mate's attention. In its habitat of tall grasses, the male florican can hope to catch a female's sight only when airborne. The jump is combined with an aerial display of white wings that contrast with the dark body, and it is this contrast that the lady likes. A large tuft of neck feathers too is unfurled and the florican puts in his hundred per cent in every leap before he lands.

Floricans belong to the family of bustards, among the heaviest of flying birds. Bengal Floricans are critically endangered because of habitat loss.

Amur Falcons galore!

The raptor holding the Guinness World Record for the longest migratory voyage, the charming Amur Falcon undertakes an epic journey from Manchuria in China to Southern Africa each year, stopping over in Northeast India to refuel. The arrival of these falcons in Northeast India coincides perfectly with the emergence of alates, winged termites that are a preferred snack. A number of villages such as Doyang in Nagaland, that used to hunt these migrating falcons for the table on a massive scale, have now turned into protected havens for tens of thousands of these record-breaking guests. Here, you'll even find structures named in honour of the species – Amur Falcon Homestay, Amur Falcon Beauty Salon, to name a few!

Expert hunters on the wing, Amur Falcons go after smaller prey, mostly insects and small birds. After this brief stopover, they traverse the Arabian Sea all the way to the African coast.

An Ashy-crowned Sparrow Lark's tweedling parabola

The Ashy-crowned Sparrow Lark is very sober in appearance, a characteristic the bird completely betrays when wooing his mate! He sings a chirruping song, soaring up to a height, and then slowly glides down with closed wings before rising again, sketching a series of invisible parabolas in the air. This undulating and almost drunken display makes for an engaging performance, both for the lady sparrow lark and the bird-watcher. Each time the performer descends, he gives out a long, continuous whistle.

Whistling, in the bird world, is to impress and never to tease.

A Gould's Sunbird collects nectar

India's answer to the hummingbirds of the New World, sunbirds are a delight to watch. Dazzling in metallic colours and ever-active, the male Gould's Sunbird seeks nectar and small insects. Rapid, buzzing beats of its tiny wings carry its nimble body swiftly from flower to flower, and the sunbird feeds as comfortably mid-air as you would while standing on your feet!

Ornithologist Nicholas Vigors named this sunbird after Elizabeth Gould, ornithological illustrator and wife of the eminent ornithologist John Gould.

Bar-headed Geese head for the Himalayas

When Bar-headed Geese migrate from frozen mountainous lakes in Central Asia to wetlands in India every winter, an insurmountable obstacle stands in the way – the mighty Himalayas. But equipped with strong wings and a sophisticated circulatory system with specialized haemoglobin that enables them to breathe at heights where hypoxia would kill most other birds, the geese take this challenge head-on. The higher the geese fly, the faster the wind current propels them over and beyond the mountains. Bar-headed Geese have even been recorded flying over Mount Everest. One of the highest flying birds in the world, this species sure believes in raising the bar unrealistically high!

A Bar-tailed Treecreeper creeps up a deodar

A treecreeper is a joy to watch, that is, if your eye is keen enough to spot this cryptically coloured bird. The Bar-tailed Treecreeper inhabits the oak and deodar forests of the Himalayas where it forages on tree trunks. Flying to the base of a tall tree, it progresses intently to the top, hopping in spiral arcs, while expertly probing cracks and crevices on the bark for insects and their larvae with its long bill. Once the tree top is reached, it flies to the base of a neighbouring tree, gleefully repeating the process.

A Barn Swallow's summer home

Angular wings and a deeply forked tail make the Barn Swallow an agile aerial hunter. Capable of sharp and sudden mid-air twists in pursuit of flies, a swallow's hunt is quite the spectacle. But summer in the Himalayan foothills brings about an even more remarkable phenomenon. From temples to shops, restaurants to houses, post offices to police stations, Barn Swallows are seen at every nook and corner, seeking a safe spot to construct cup-shaped nests from mud pellets. Nesting in human habitation assures safety from predators such as hawks that are too wary to venture in, while the generally large-hearted mountainfolk find it only natural to share space with winged friends, only occasionally regretting the growing family's toilet habits.

An Asian Barn Owl Hunts

The Barn Owl has razor talons and a sharply hooked bill – like any other bird of prey. But silence is the owl's most lethal weapon. Scanning a a field or a townscape from its favoured perch, it uses its acute hearing to spot its target. The asymmetrically placed ears pinpoint the location of its prey, which the owl gathers by tilting its head from time to time to allow sound waves to reach both ears simultaneously. Once the scurrying rodent is spotted, the next thing it meets is its death because every part of the hunt, from the take-off to the pounce, is executed in pitch-perfect silence, made possible by the noise-cancelling arrangement and structure of the owl's fight feathers. The rodent is then carried to the owl's nest, typically in holes along the walls of old buildings, where it is dispatched to a hungry family. Barn Owls can kill more than twenty mice in a single night and are regarded worldwide as one of the most effective non-toxic pest control services!

A Bay-backed Shrike butchers

In a patch of scrub, a Bay-backed Shrike spots a fat, juicy Calotes lizard. Its thick bill is employed, and the lizard is caught. But the prey in this case is just about as big as the predator itself, and a tough customer to tackle. So what does the bird do? It puts its favourite perch – the thorny acacia tree – to good use. Choosing a sharp yet sturdy thorn, the shrike impales its quarry through and through, before dislodging and consuming it bit by bit. Shrikes have been recorded killing a variety of prey in this fashion, including birds, snakes and even rodents, which are often bigger than themselves! This formidable behaviour, coupled with its black mask, has earned it nicknames such as 'butcher-bird' and 'bandit'.

Black-breasted Parrotbills crack some grass

Except when whistling its fluty song from a perch to claim territory, the secretive Black-breasted Parrotbill seldom presents itself. The tall grasses it inhabits (easily taller than an adult human being, and some even taller than elephants) further enhance its skulky lifestyle. Despite resembling a parrot in appearance, owing to its curved nutcracker-like bill, the Black-breasted Parrotbill is actually a relative of the insectivorous warblers, being an insect-eater itself. So, is the nutcracker-shaped bill an evolutionary folly? Quite the contrary! Long and tough reed stems are clasped tight in this hooked apparatus and cracked open to expose insect larvae residing within. The loud cracking is often more audible than the bird itself!

Endemic to the Brahmaputra floodplains and grasslands in the foothills of the Eastern Himalayas, the species is severely threatened by habitat loss.

Bonebreaker: Bearded Vulture

The Bearded Vulture or Lammergeier of the Himalayas eats carrion like every other vulture. But what it does next takes scavenging to another level. Carrying a huge bone in its talons, the vulture soars until it spots a perfect rocky surface. In a move executed with military precision, it drops the bone bang on the rock, cracking it open, and then descends to feast on the exposed marrow – a source of food and nutrition inaccessible to other birds. If a Lammergeier were reading this, it would certainly have raised an objection to how easy the manoeuvre has been made to sound, because this skill – involving a great deal of mathematical learning – takes about seven years to master!

Hello, Beautiful: Beautiful Nuthatch

The Beautiful Nuthatch is a resident of montane forests of the Northeast. Nuthatches, much like treecreepers, forage in the crevices and cracks of tree trunks, but move in spirals from the apex downwards. While insects and their larvae hiding in epiphytes and bark crevices are its usual fare, nuthatches also wedge nuts between cracks in the bark, hacking the seeds to split them open – a trait which gives them their name.

Nuthatches, like woodpeckers, are cavity nesters, nesting in tree holes. The Beautiful Nuthatch can often be found associating with other birds in mixed-species feeding flocks.

Bird or reed? Black Bittern

The Black Bittern, a close relative of herons, hunts fish and frogs in reed beds. This patient hunter waits for its prey to swim within striking range, before darting at it in a snap with its spear-like bill. But defence, not attack, is the bittern's true specialty. The moment it spots a threat, such as a harrier examining the reeds for prey, the bittern stretches its long neck and freezes. Dark serrated lines on its neck mimic the patterns of the reeds, helping it blend perfectly with its habitat. It does not end there; some bitterns improvise further – swaying their necks gently to mimic the movements of reed stems in the breeze!

A Baya Weaver weaves

If you are a male Baya Weaver and you do not possess a master's in architecture, you're doomed to be a bachelor for life. For, a successful breeding season is assured only if a weaver is capable of building elaborate, pendulous nests. The complex nest can take over 500 foraging trips to complete. But before that, tying the perfect first knot as the nest's foundation is the key to building the rest of it successfully, a skill that takes considerable experience to master. Once the nest is partially built, the male begins to advertise by calling out to potential mates. When a female passer-by takes an interest, she first inspects the structure carefully, and only if she finds it conducive to raise her young does she accept the proposal. The rest of the nest is built by the pair together. Baya nesting colonies are usually built close to water bodies to reduce the risk of predation by snakes.

Hellboy: Black Drongo

Forest fires destroy any animal or plant in their way, but they are a Black Drongo's ally. An agile hunter on the wing, owing to its forked tail, the drongo has mastered the art of using fires to its benefit, by strategically hawking insects that are disturbed by the flames. Although essentially diurnal in habit, the versatile drongo can often be seen in the late hours of the night, hunting insects that are attracted by street lights. Well known for its ferocity, it also actively mobs birds of prey much larger than itself, dive-bombing and harassing them until they move away from its brood. Several species such as doves and bulbuls love nesting in the safety of the Black Drongo's vicinity. Its courage and vigilance have earned this bird the nickname 'kotwal', meaning a police constable!

Brunchlings: Black Eagle

The Black Eagle's long wings with deep and widely splayed 'fingers' not only make it a graceful flier to watch, but also enable the bird to glide slowly over the canopy as it scans for a meal. The act of procuring it, however, is anything but graceful. This raptor's favourite snack is nestlings of other birds. Once a nest is spotted, the eagle descends, and soars away with the entire nest clasped tightly in its talons. On returning to the comfort of its perch, the contents of the nest, be they eggs or chicks, are gulped down one by one.

Black Eagles inhabit hill forests, and are quite frequently encountered in the Western Ghats, the Himalayas and the Northeast.

A Black Kite steals

It is remarkable how a tiny tweak of evolution can be a species' defining talent. In the Black Kite's case, this is the fork in its tail. The sheer range of flight stunts this feature supports makes the Black Kite the top scavenger in an urban setting. Gliding above a busy fish market, the kite spots a freshly discarded fish head. A sudden swoop, dive and snatch, and the fish head is in the kite's possession before anyone can notice! It is the forked tail that enables complicated aerial manoeuvres – swift and sharp turns to dodge power pylons, transmission lines and overhanging roofs. Black Kites are bold enough to use mobile towers as nesting spots.

Although kites are well-equipped to hunt, and do hunt frequently, they prefer to scavenge from slaughterhouses, garbage dumps and road kills. Who doesn't like fast food?

An unpleasant surprise, courtesy the Black-necked Stork

Still as wood, a Black-necked Stork stands at the lakefront, minding its business. The stork has been standing there for hours. What harm could it possibly do? Having made that erroneous judgement, a Common Coot swims past the stork. Before it can blink, the stork's dagger-shaped bill jabs its body, reducing the coot to breakfast.

While a Black-necked Stork's usual quarry is fish, frogs and water snakes, it does not hesitate to startle unsuspecting ducks, waterhens and even herons from time to time!

A Black-Winged Kite hunts

Perched on an open-ended branch, a Black-winged Kite scans the field below, bobbing its tail up and down in the excitement of the hunt . What follows is pure aeronautical magic. The raptor hovers with its eyes glued to the target and body pinned to the air, with wings fluttering to keep it in position; sharp eyes follow every move of its prey, calculating the exact moment to dive. Once the prey is within attacking range, a swift swoop and the kite disappears into the scrubs, emerging seconds later with a rodent in its talons. As you may have guessed, this effective cleansing of rodents from our fields is a great service to both the farmer and the reader of this book!

The Good Shepherd: Cattle Egret

Visit any field or marsh across India and you will find buffaloes accompanied by their winged allies, aptly named Cattle Egrets. Unlike their wetland cousins – herons and other egrets that are more aquatic in habit – Cattle Egrets feed on land. They trot alongside cattle, darting at insects such as crickets and grasshoppers that are flushed by the hooves. A versatile bird, it has adapted to live in the company of several 'hosts' such as cows, horses, wild buffalo, deer, and even elephants and rhinoceroses, and can be seen catching a free ride on their backs. The hosts too don't mind the 'passenger' as the egret helps them get rid of flies and maggots on their hides.

Cattle Egrets have kept pace with technology and have learnt to follow tractors ploughing fields to catch insects disturbed by the machines. Draped in white the rest of the year, these birds assume a gorgeous orange breeding plumage when monsoon arrives.

A Brown Dipper dips

Dippers live along fast-flowing streams in the mountains, where they hunt aquatic insects and their larvae. The Brown Dipper's stout build isn't exactly the typical profile for an aquatic bird, but this songbird from the Himalayas is blessed with some remarkable aquatic adaptations. Its short, stubby wings are strongly muscled and act as flippers underwater. Its feet may not be webbed like other waterbirds, but have strong digits to enable a firm grip on the edges of rocks, where it perches and hunts from. A nictitating membrane masks its eyes and a nasal flap covers the nostrils underwater, helping the dipper hold its breath in water for upto thirty seconds! Its dense plumage is kept waterproof by secretions from large preen glands. Its feathers also trap air, creating a bubble around the bird's body when underwater.

The dipper lacks an athletic build, yet is a seasoned diver. Breaking stereotypes is another trait the dipper seems to specialize in!

A Brown Fish-Owl fishes

Brown Fish-Owls spend the day roosting in wooded cover, often mobbed by smaller birds like babblers and parakeets. Nightfall is when the thrill begins. Atypical for an owl, the fish owl does not usually hunt by silently swooping upon its victim. It adopts a strategy more akin to a wader rather than an owl! Descending upon a rock, it scans the shallow water for fish, frogs and crabs. It then wades through the water, skimming the surface with its feet. The sharp, deadly talons are used to grasp and carry its slithery aquatic prey to the owl's preferred perch, where the snack is devoured in peace.

Hindsight: Collared Owlet

Despite its diminutive look, the Collared Owlet has the reputation of being a serial killer on the prowl. Dreaded by birds much larger than itself, it ambushes them in the forests of the Himalayas. Its cryptic colouration helps it to close in on a flock of Bhutan Laughingthrushes, and a swift aerial ambush is carried out when the sentries are off their guard. As the bird carries its meal to a perch, the killer reveals a bizarre defence mechanism – an intimidating pair of false eyes at the back of its head, that deters a larger predator from approaching it! In these hill forests, birds can often be seen associating with several other species in mixed-feeding flocks, to safeguard themselves from this bird-killer.

A Common Tailorbird weaves

One of our most common garden birds, the Common Tailorbird is an enthusiastic vocalist, filling the neighbourhood with its disyllabic 'cheuwi-cheuwi' song . But it is in the monsoon, when the tailorbird breeds, that its eponymous skill is revealed. When it chances upon the perfect cluster of leaves, the bird punches quick holes along the leaves' edges with its needle-like bill. Using plant fibre (or even spider-silk) the holes are sewn with remarkable dexterity until a cradle of leaves emerges, and the edges are then stitched tight. A soft bed is made within the cradle, into which the eggs are laid.

Tailorbirds are very active insectivores, and naturally, effective pest controllers for your garden. Similar weaving techniques are also practised by some species of prinias, close cousins of the tailors.

Coppersmith at work: Coppersmith Barbet

The Coppersmith Barbet's metallic 'tuk-tuk-tuk' call, reminiscent of a metalworker striking a sheet of metal, gives it its name. Closely related to woodpeckers, the barbet uses its thick, strong bill to excavate cavities in trees in which it nests. The bird sports a lavish contrast of red, yellow and black on its face, while the rest of its body is foliage-green. The barbet can be seen perched on open branches, sunning itself before it sets about on the day's chores. An ardent eater of fruits, particularly figs, the barbet's bill can accommodate a considerable bunch before it flies off to its nest with the day's collection. Barbets are important dispersers of fig seeds in Indian forests, helping them spread and regenerate.

A Crested Goshawk strikes

Hunting amidst dense rainforest foliage is a complicated task, but the Crested Goshawk is built for the job. Compared to other birds of prey, its wings are much shorter and broader, giving it the ability to manoeuvre through forest cover even in fast flight. A long tail steers the hunter's aerial turns, and a network of stripes and bars on its body help it blend with the dense vegetation. Before its target can make an escape, the long, thick claws – which give the bird its generic name, *Accipiter* (meaning 'a hawk that grasps' in Latin) – have already done their job. The prey is then shredded to pieces in the comfort of a secretive perch.

Crested Goshawks are found in well-wooded forests, especially in the Western Ghats and the Northeast.

A Royal Hunt: Changeable Hawk-Eagle

The regal Changeable Hawk-Eagle, aptly called 'Shahbaaz' (The King of Eagles) in Urdu, scans the forest from a vantage point, perched upright on a Sal tree at the forest's edge. A Red Junglefowl makes the mistake of exposing itself to the eagle's gaze. Both predator and prey make their moves, and the race begins. While the pheasant is quick on its feet through the bushes, the hunter is equipped with superior flexibility and agility on the wing; its short and broad wing proportions enabling sharp manoeuvres through the foliage. Once outrun, the pheasant is pinned to the ground with the eagle's strong legs and ineluctable talons. His majesty's lunch is served!

The Changeable Hawk-Eagle is capable of hunting birds much larger than itself, such as the Indian Peafowl!

Crested Serpent-Eagle versus Cobra

One of India's commonest forest raptors, the Crested Serpent-Eagle, as the name implies, is a snake-eater. Trees at the edge of forests are its usual perch, from where it scans clearings or dry riverbeds for snakes. While its usual prey of small, non-venomous snakes are briskly carried off in flight, larger prey such as the cobra demands more valour.

The killer swoops down, startling the snake. A show of headgear precedes the battle, with the cobra erecting its hood and its avian adversary flaring its feathered crest, both attempting to appear larger and more formidable. As the cobra strikes, the eagle's reflexes must be swift enough to not only avoid the venomous fangs but to also pin the snake down by the head. The sharp, hooked bill is then deployed to behead the serpent and immobilize its body, before carrying it away for a pair of hungry eaglets.

An Oriental Darter darts

'Snakebird' is an apt nickname for the darter. It may seem awkward at the surface, but once underwater, the darter transforms into a serpent! Its webbed feet propel the bird towards its chosen prey, mostly fish, while the incredibly long neck directs the dart-shaped bill that efficiently stabs the body of the fish through and through. When the darter resurfaces, it tosses its meal up in the air before gulping it down.

To increase buoyancy and accelerate their pursuit of aquatic prey, darters and their close cousins, the cormorants, have lost the water-repelling properties of their feathers. As a result, they hold their wings open in the sun to dry their feathers for hours after each dive!

Saliva and Sonar: Edible-nest Swiftlet

Cave systems are home to some of the most extraordinary living organisms, and the caves of the Andaman and Nicobar Islands host one such surprise. The Edible-nest Swiftlet nests in these caves, constructing cup-shaped nests made of layers of hardened saliva! These nests are harvested and cooked as 'bird's nest soup', a Southeast Asian delicacy, giving the species its name.

But living in caves needs evolutionary innovation. Although the bird hunts in daylight, it uses echolocation to guide itself back to its nest in the pitch-dark caves! Cave swiftlets are among the few birds known to science that use echolocation.

A Eurasian Spoonbill's table-tact

It is common knowledge that the spoonbill gets its name from its spoon-shaped mandibles. But what exactly does it use this pair of spoons for? Unlike most other long-billed waders that probe underwater for food, the spoonbill forages by moving its partly open bill in sweeping motions. The bill, apart from being uniquely shaped, is also equipped with enhanced tactile sensors. As it sweeps through the water in arcs, a snail or a crustacean passing by is detected thanks to the bill's sensory superpower, and the spoon snaps shut. The snail is then tossed up in the air and gulped.

Another sub-continental wader, the critically endangered Spoon-billed Sandpiper, also uses the same technique to forage.

A Eurasian Wryneck does the twist

The Eurasian Wryneck is a woodpecker that is not quite a woodpecker. Instead of chipping at tree bark, it often feeds on the ground, pecking at anthills and termite mounds. Usually, it uses a pre-existing cavity to nest, instead of excavating its own (the wryneck does not breed in India and is a winter migrant to the subcontinent). But it is another bizarre adaptation that gives it its name. When threatened, the wryneck performs an outlandish threat display, contorting and twisting its head from side to side and hissing – almost as if mimicking a snake! Having baffled its predator completely, the bird takes wing, flying to the safety of a nearby tree. This unusual behaviour also led to the bird's use in witchcraft in medieval times, and gave it its Latin name *Jynx*, a reference to the act of placing a jinx on someone by employing black magic.

A Great Indian Bustard courts

Being critically endangered and on the very brink of extinction means that it is not always possible to find a mate. But when the Great Indian Bustard does find one, he does not shy away from proclaiming his love out loud, emitting a loud, resonating 'boom' which can be heard for half a kilometre! As the polygynous male mates in a lek, the call not only attracts the attention of the ladies but also serves as a signal to rival males to keep away.

Is any Rajasthani performance ever complete without a show of ornaments? The courting state bird of Rajasthan inflates a large, feathery gular pouch, forming a fluffy bag beneath its chin. The tail feathers are also cocked up and folded on the back as the cock marches gallantly towards the hen.

Great Indian Bustards are slow breeders and lay only a single egg on the ground. The species faces an imminent threat of extinction because of habitat loss, and collisions with power transmission lines and windmills. It could well be the first bird to go extinct in independent India if immediate action is not taken.

Marching in muck: Greater Adjutants

A few kilometres from the city of Guwahati, a municipal corporation garbage truck arriving at a massive landfill is greeted by hundreds of odd-looking storks. Sporting a grey-black feathered suit complemented by a bright orange gular pouch that hangs awkwardly like a badly worn necktie, a messy ruff of white feathers and a vulture-like pink, naked head, Greater Adjutants scavenge in these landfills, waiting for the truck to unload 'the day's catch'. Greater Adjutants get their name, or rather their military rank, from their stiff and pompous marching gait. Scavengers by nature, they make a meal out of anything remotely edible – from decaying carcasses at the landfill to offal being dumped by the trucks. While the storks have no problems feeding alongside municipal workers and ragpickers, they are wary of 'outsiders' – birdwatchers, photographers and scientists! Recent improvements in sanitation and waste management are believed to be the cause of decline of this endangered species, numbering just over a thousand worldwide. Their largest population is in Assam, and the other in Cambodia.

Unconventional Cuckoo: Greater Coucal

Like most cuckoos, Greater Coucals are very vocal. Their low-pitched, resonant 'oop-oop-oop' duets reverberate in the woods, giving their presence away. But they differ from their cuckoo cousins in making their own nests and caring for their young. Ferocious and versatile predators, they prey on a wide range of creatures including large insects, lizards, frogs, small snakes, birds' eggs and nestlings – all of which are hunted at every level of the foliage or on the ground. I have personally observed a coucal climbing on top of a bird box in my house, making a meal out of two House Sparrow nestlings! The coral-red eyes enhance both their beauty and menacing appearance.

A Greater Painted-Snipe speed dates

The panels may seem to depict regular courtship display until you arrive at the third image. Breaking stereotypes by reversing gender roles is this bird's forte. The more striking and colourful female performs a courtship display to attract a mate, cocking her tail and fanning dotted feathers. She even aggressively defends her mate from the advances of other females. Once the nest is built and the eggs are laid, she leaves the eggs to the care of the father and finds another date.

Jacanas and phalaropes, which are found in the subcontinent, also reverse gender roles.

Fooling your friends: Greater Racquet-tailed Drongo

Ask any Indian who the best mimic in the country is and you are likely to hear the names of comedians Johny Lever or Sunil Grover. But Lever and Grover impersonate human beings. The Greater Racquet-tailed Drongo takes mimicry to a whole new level by mimicking other species! Exactly why the drongo mimics is still being researched, but it is believed that it brings different birds together and initiates the formation of mixed species feeding flocks that enable birds to find food and keep an eye out for predators with greater success. But our prankster has more tricks up its sleeve. The drongo's repertoire of mimicry also includes false alarms and the calls of birds of prey, which causes panic among the mixed flocks. As the drongo imitates a goshawk (a predator of birds), a startled scimitar-babbler drops a winged insect that it had just caught, which is then swiftly scooped up by the drongo. No one spots the bluff in this game of poker.

A Grey Wagtail's wagday out

Just looking at a wagtail is enough to lift one's spirits on a gloomy day. The constant waggling of the long tail makes you wonder where the bird gets all the cheer and the energy from! Grey Wagtails visit peninsular India every winter, flying in from their breeding grounds in the Himalayas and beyond, often visiting the same wintering site annually. This could be a narrow forest stream or a pond in an urban garden where aquatic insects abound. Walking along the waterbody in its characteristic merry manner, the wagtail grabs quick bites from the surface. If disturbed, it takes to the wing instantly, its undulating flight radiating the same cheer and energy as its gait!

Courting with colour: Himalayan Monal

Among the world's most colourful birds, the male Himalayan Monal has captivated every bird lover with its resplendent plumage. But female monals demand more effort – such as an elaborate show of embellishments. Although all male pheasants specialize in courtship displays, the monal's iridescence makes its performance the most dazzling among pheasants. The show begins with the erection of the bird's copper-green crest. The metallic blue wings are then unfurled. As the tail is raised, the contrasting white rump grabs the lady's eyeballs even as the fanning movement of the orange tail feathers enthrals her. When colour is what you seek, and just about every colour from the palette is what you get, there is not much reason to say no!

The Himalayan Monal is the national bird of Nepal and the state bird of Uttarakhand.

A leaf comes to life: Indian Nightjar

The cryptically coloured Indian Nightjar spends the day pretending to be just another dead leaf amid all the dried-up leaf litter on the ground. Its impeccable camouflage ensures a sound daytime nap, saving up all the energy the nightjar needs for a buzzing nightlife. As dusk approaches, the Indian Nightjar begins to emit its characteristic 'chuk-chuk-chukrrrruk' call, reminiscent of a bouncing ping-pong ball. Its long-winged, raptor-like profile, large eyes and broad bill make it an adept nighttime hunter on the wing – hawking moths and crickets in flight. Come dawn, the bird turns back into a dead leaf.

Hopping along: Ground Tit

Life is challenging and resources limited in the roof of the world, the Tibetan Plateau. But a unique ground-dwelling bird, the Gound Tit, is well adapted to eke out a living in the cold desert. A delight to the birder, this bird, also known as the Groundpecker, hops as if it is wearing spring-fitted shoes! Its long hoopoe-like bill is used to dig into and probe crevices and cracks in the ground for arthropod prey. Droppings of yaks are regularly turned over to flush insects that feed on the dung. The Ground Tit nests in burrows in the mud. Its puzzling morphology has been the cause of great confusion among taxonomists; the bird was historically classified with crows and jays until molecular studies of its DNA revealed its close links to tits.

A House Sparrow couple's to-do list

Our most familiar neighbourhood bird, the House Sparrow, makes itself at home wherever opportunity presents, such as the electric metre box that hosts a pair in my house every season. Sparrows are busy birds, especially when raising a brood. A quick drink and a dip, and the pair is ready to take on the summer sun. First stop, the closest granary for breakfast, where the opportunists gather to raid a torn rice sack. Having had their fill, they head to a nearby garden to hunt for some protein for their chicks, usually juicy earthworms. The chicks are fed at regular intervals, and both sexes make extremely dedicated parents, taking turns to tend to the brood and defend the nest from potential intruders. Congregating in the nearby field for a dust bath is usually how the gregarious sparrows call it a day.

A Hume's Leaf-Warbler flits in the leaves

Leaf warblers can be tinier than the leaves they forage in, and their dull green plumage offers appropriate camouflage, but their extreme restlessness gives them away. The Hume's Leaf-Warbler can be identified by the two bright wing bars on its drab-green wings and its disyllabic 'chew-ip' notes, uttered cheerfully as it flits about in the leaves. This vocalization, pleasing to the human ear, is, in fact, a threat to a territorial rival! Hovering around foliage, it seeks insects and grubs tucked in the corners, catching and consuming them swiftly before moving on to the next cluster of leaves.

For their size, the warblers undertake remarkable migratory journeys. The Hume's Leaf-Warbler visits northern and central India from the mountains of Central Asia every winter!

Synchronized swimmers: Indian Cormorants

The Indian Cormorant's webbed feet, strong wings and streamlined profile give it just the right design needed for underwater athletics. A specialized fisher, the cormorant has lost the water-repelling properties of its feathers, so as to decrease buoyancy during underwater hunts and enhance the pursuit of fish. But the cormorants unveil their true wonder when fishing as a team. The gregarious fishers form a coalition, swimming in awe-inspiring synchrony in pursuit of schools of fish, rapidly steering them towards the shore. Once cornered, the fish become easy targets not just for the cormorants but also for an opportunist egret or heron waiting at the shore! After fishing marathons, the birds head to their perches, holding their wings open in the sun for long hours to dry the feathers.

An Indian Pitta forages

Heard more often than seen, the dazzling Indian Pitta's loud, melodious two-toned whistle announces its presence. Known as 'Navrang' in Hindi, the pitta sports a splendid array of colours. Its characteristic long legs are a specialized feature for feeding on the ground. The pitta hops about in leaf litter, frequently turning dead leaves to seek worms, insects, small amphibians and reptiles. Once the prey is caught, it is battered on a rock or on the ground and immobilized before being consumed. The pitta constructs its sphere-shaped nest made of dead leaves and grasses on low branches or on the ground. Resident in peninsular India, the Indian Pitta migrates to northern India during summer.

An Indian Peafowl woos

A puzzling paradox to Charles Darwin, but a delight to the layviewer, the Indian Peafowl's mating dance enchants visitors from around the world. The peacock's loud, resonant mewing echoes through the forest, announcing the arrival of the monsoon as well as the bird's breeding season. As the hens gather, the cock unfolds his long resplendent uppertail coverts, which he spreads out like a shimmering, quivering fan. It is this train of feathers that determines which male wins the mating game. The polygamous cock mates with several hens in the breeding season, while the females single-handedly raise the brood.

Hoopoeing around: Common Hoopoe

The most striking feature of a hoopoe is its crest. Erected at frequent intervals, it gives the appearance of ornate tribal headgear! Often wrongly thought of as a woodpecker, the hoopoe forages on the ground, putting its long, needle-like bill to good use. It probes the ground for insects and their larvae, drilling them out when detected. Nesting in tree cavities, hoopoes are well-equipped to defend themselves against predators. The preen glands of both the incubating female and the chicks produce a foul-smelling liquid that repels attackers. The chicks are also capable of 'greeting' the approaching intruder with a spray of faeces and snake-like hisses! Sunbathing is a favourite indulgence of hoopoes, and long basking sessions, with their wings spread out and heads tilted up, are much relished by this species. A bird of simple pleasures!

An Indian Roller rolls

(Disclaimer: The stunts in this scene have been performed by trained professionals. Imitate at your own risk!)

Nothing says 'you make my world spin around' like the male Indian Roller's courtship display – a series of somersaults performed mid-air that showcase the sparkling blue spots on his indigo wings. This 'rolling' display is what gives the species its name. The lady roller obviously has a taste for raw action and picks the best stuntman among her suitors.

A perched Indian Roller is a familiar sight on a drive along the Indian countryside. Serially ridding our fields of agricultural pests, the roller is a farmer's friend and is even worshipped in parts of India.

Synchronized duet: Indian Scimitar-Babblers

Despite being skulkers by nature, Indian Scimitar-Babblers do not shy away from putting up lively duets which indicate their presence in dense evergreen forests. The male's fluty 'oop-pu-pu-pu-pu' is followed in quick succession by the female's guttural 'krukruk'! Their down-curved long bills, which give them their name, are used to pick caterpillars and insects from trees and the ground. Scimitar-Babblers are often seen associating with birds like fulvettas, drongos, woodpeckers and other babblers in mixed-species feeding flocks.

Edward Scissorbill: Indian Skimmer

Sporting a contrasting black-and-white plumage topped with a bright-red bill, the Indian Skimmer is a striking bird. But a closer look at the skimmer's bill will puzzle the observer. The lower mandible is longer than the upper! What purpose could this serve? Residents of river basins, skimmers are strong fliers. Their long wings enable them to fly low, parallel to the surface of the water, with the bill held open. The extended lower bill tip is used to skim the water's surface as the bird flies. The moment the tip comes in contact with a fish, the scissor-like bill is snapped shut.

Skimmer populations are declining rapidly because of sand mining, habitat loss and pollution of water bodies. 

The Caching Crow: Large-spotted Nutcracker

The Large-spotted or the Kashmir Nutcracker is not just any crow. A specialized feeder of pine seeds, it has developed some remarkable features. Grasping a pine cone in its talons, the nutcracker hammers it with its massive bill, breaking the shell open. Its tongue is unique in shape and structure, with two hard, keratinized structures at the tip that are used to clasp the seed and pull it out. Nutcrackers cache surplus food for use in winter, burying the extracted seed into the soil. Crows of all kinds around the world are renowned for their intelligence, and the nutcracker takes this a step further. Its brain is equipped with long-term spatial memory, and it can remember up to 70 per cent of its cache sites correctly using physical landmarks, even when they are covered in snow! And no prizes for guessing what happens to the caches it forgets – yes, they grow into pine forests! This intricate relationship between the 'farmer' and the crop is crucial for the survival of both.

Flamingo flashmob: Lesser Flamingos

Flamingos possess several unique traits: elongated necks and legs, bills equipped for filter-feeding, slender and elegant profiles, and flashy pink plumage acquired from beta-carotenoid pigments in their diet of algae and crustaceans. And if there is anything as flamboyant as their appearance, it is their courtship display. When the breeding season commences, groups comprising both males and females march together, flagging their heads rhythmically from side to side in what looks like a choreographed techno dance! The stylized stunt is followed by pairs courting each other with graceful 'wing salutes', their elongated necks held up and their wings spread out. The mates then courteously bow, with the tail and the black flight feathers pointing skyward, before consummating their bond.

Gregarious by nature, flamingos nest in colonies, where each pair builds nests on mud mounds and both sexes contribute equally towards raising the single offspring.

A Lesser Florican leaps

If the long jump is the Bengal Florican's forte, its cousin, the Lesser Florican is a high jump gold medalist! Floricans live amid tall grasses and the only way to grab a female's eyeballs in their habitat is through an ingenious courtship display. To make sure he gets noticed, the long-legged male suddenly takes off from the grass vertically while emitting a croaking call, and disappears into the grass again as he descends. The leap is repeated every three minutes or so. The higher he is able to jump, the fitter he appears to his prospective mate – a prerequisite for finding a partner.

Lesser Floricans are threatened by habitat loss, just like other bustards in India, and have declined rapidly in recent times.

Doting Dabchick: Little Grebe

Well-adapted for aquatic life, the Little Grebe or Dabchick is an excellent diver. Its strong webbed feet act as underwater propellers as it pursues tiny fish, crustaceans and frogs. These feet also help the grebe paddle over the water surface to make a quick getaway when threatened. Grebes are known for making floating nests, constructed from grasses and reeds. They are devoted and protective parents. Although the precocial chicks are independent and capable of swimming at birth, they are fed by the parents and even carried on their backs. It sure helps to have a luxury cruiser for a parent!

Bouquet Bachata: Great Crested Grebes

'Complement every step of your dancemate's with yours' – these aren't just a Bachata instructor's elementary lessons, but also the choreography handbook for Great Crested Grebes. The grebe couple's courtship dance is an elaborate performance, with the pair facing each other and mirroring every step. As one partner's head tilts to the left, so does the other's. When she looks right, so does he. When he shakes her head, ruffling the black-and-orange frill of feathers that the birds grow in their breeding plumage around their necks, she follows suit. Then the pair dives, emerging with a bouquet of vegetation plucked from the lakebed in their beaks. And then comes the chassé. Pedaling vigorously, the couple moves closer until they face each other almost vertically, breasts pressed together, as if to garland each other with the weed necklaces! As this mesmerizing performance unfolds, an onlooker cannot help but imagine a calm, sensuous melody playing in the background.

Great Crested Grebes are winter migrants to India, breeding only in a few sites in the north-west.

Family Man: Malabar Pied Hornbill

In nature, one cannot afford to complain about working overtime, especially when you are the breadwinner for your entire family. Like most hornbills, the nesting female Malabar Pied Hornbill locks herself up in a tree hollow, sealing the cavity using a cement made up of her droppings, mud and fruit pulp. This ensures maximum protection for her chicks. As long as she is sealed inside, the male hornbill, one of nature's most dedicated fathers, works round the clock to provide supplies to the mother and the chicks through a narrow slit in the nest cavity. A hornbill's diet includes a wide range of food including insects, reptiles, fruits and even other nestlings! They harbour a soft spot for figs, which they also disperse across great distances – no surprise then that hornbills are said to be capable of regenerating entire forests!

After the chicks have grown in size, the female breaks the seal open, joining the father in raising the young until they are ready to leave the nest.

Melody in the mist: Malabar Whistling Thrush

You know you are in the Western Ghats when the melodious, jovial whistle of the Malabar Whistling Thrush reverberates through the hills. The human quality of its whistle led Dr Salim Ali to nickname the bird 'whistling schoolboy'! When not exercising its vocal cords, the whistling thrush forages on the ground amidst leaf litter. Hopping on its long feet, it overturns piles of leaves to scout for prey, usually small crabs and snails. Using its strong bill that has a slight hook at the tip, the thrush batters the prey on hard surfaces of rocks or fallen branches. The shell is cracked open and the soft body of the victim is devoured before the bird heads to its favourite perch to launch into another song. It is almost as if this gifted vocalist is on a mission to fill the hillside air with music!

Mounds on the island: Nicobar Megapode

Nicobar Megapodes, or Scrubfowls, always seem preoccupied with digging and scraping the soil. But there's a reason why they have such large feet and strong claws ('megapode' in Latin means just that – large feet). They are the only birds that incubate eggs not with body heat but with the help of microbes! Megapodes build large mounds by piling together soil and vegetation that soon starts to decay. When a sufficient height is reached, the eggs are laid in the mound and covered. The energy released from microbial activity in the decomposing matter incubates the eggs, so the parents don't need to warm them with their own bodies. Megapode chicks are precocial, capable of running around and feeding themselves immediately after they hatch! The species is found only on some islands of the Nicobar archipelago.

Nanogardener: Nilgiri Flowerpecker

The smallest bird in the book (and in India), and a rather drab one at that, yet the Nilgiri Flowerpecker garners one of the longest illustrated sequences. That is because the love story between the flowerpecker and the mistletoe plant is anything but drab! The mistletoe, an epiphyte growing on other trees, is served by the little flowerpecker in two ways – pollination and seed dispersal. As the bird pecks at the mistletoe flower for nectar, the petals pop open scattering pollen all over the bird's face, which it dutifully deposits on the next flower it visits. Ripe mistletoe fruits too are the flowerpecker's beloved snack. The bird squeezes the fruit in its tiny bill to consume the pulp and then rubs the beak against the bark to get rid of the sticky seed. If ingested, the fruit passes through the gut rapidly, prompting the bird to wipe its rear end awkwardly against the bark to detach the seed enclosed in sticky sap. Both these events happen to be part of nature's grand horticultural plan – planting the mistletoe seed directly on the host tree!

Rainbow bullet: Oriental Dwarf Kingfisher

Sporting a vibrant hue of colours, the dazzling Oriental Dwarf Kingfisher is an obvious favourite of birdwatchers and photographers (not to mention, illustrators!). When such a colourful bird darts across the damp rainforest in typical kingfisher fashion, it appears like a fragment of a rainbow shot from a gun. Dwarf kingfishers live along streams in dense forests, where they hunt crabs, frogs and lizards. Like most kingfishers, this species too nests in tunnels excavated along the banks of streams, laying three to five eggs. Dwarf kingfishers breed during the monsoon.

An Oriental Honey-Buzzard goes honey-hunting

The Oriental Honey-Buzzard is something of a cross between a raptor and a pigeon. It sports an eagle-like body with a pigeon-like head, a long, slender neck and feet covered in thick scales – these are all adaptations for raiding beehives; a habit that gives the bird its name. Much like an eagle pouncing on a hare, the honey-buzzard attacks beehives. The scales on its bare feet and around the bill protect the bird from bee stings, and the long neck and thin bill enable better access into the hive. Chunks from the hive are broken off and carried away from its furious and agitated defenders to a safe perch where the bird feasts on the bee larvae.

Birds may lack teeth but this honey-hunter sure has a sweet tooth!

'Breastfeeding' dad: Painted Sandgrouse

Sandgrouses, close relatives of doves and pigeons, live in deserts and scrubs that have limited access to water. While the adult birds can fly to the closest waterbody to get a drink, their chicks born in ground nests must stay put as they depend on their camouflage to escape the eyes of a predator. This is where the tiger-striped father steps in. Male sandgrouses are equipped with special absorbent feathers on their breasts that soak and retain water. The father, after quenching his thirst, puffs these breast feathers out and dips them in the water generously, collecting every drop of 'liquid gold' he can. He then flies off directly to the nest so as not to waste a single drop. The chicks 'peck' the water off his breast feathers, just like a suckling mammal. The Painted Sandgrouse lives in arid regions.

Pirates of the Indian Seas: Arctic Jaegers

Thugs of Hindostan could have been a far more entertaining film had it revolved around the life of a true maritime pirate of coastal India, the Arctic Jaeger aka Arctic Skua. Although the Jaegers are capable of hunting, most of their food comes from kleptoparasitism: stealing food from other birds like gulls and terms. On spotting a tern make a successful dive, the Jaeger starts mobbing its victim. The Jaeger's bulky body renders it a fearsome adversary; its falcon-like wings and sharp turn it into an agile fighter pilot in pursuit, and its sheer relentlessness makes it a downright nuisance for the tern. The harassment continues until the tern is forced to drop its catch, swiftly stolen by the thief.

Under daddy's wings: Pheasant-tailed Jacana

Pheasant-tailed Jacana chicks are brought up by single fathers. Their mothers set out in search of new mates, leaving the clutch in the father's care. It helps that the chicks are precocial, capable of independently executing what jacanas are famous for – walking over lotus leaves on the surface of ponds and lakes using their long, slender feet as they forage for aquatic insects. But the chicks still need protection from predators. As a Marsh Harrier circles over the lake seeking prey, the handsome jacana father sounds the alarm. The chicks rush straight towards their father, hiding under his wings, quite literally, until the threat has passed. Although the chicks take refuge in the father's warm embrace, their feet are too big to be tucked under him. Their dangling legs give the father the appearance of a four-footed bird.

Reverse-beaked: Pied Avocet

A downcurved bill is a relatively common feature in birds – ibises, curlews and a few other waders sport them. But in the Pied Avocet, the feature is reversed, earning its genus the name *Recurvirostra*, meaning reverse-turned bill. Winter migrants to the Indian coasts, avocets gather in flocks in shallow, brackish waters. The upturned bill is used as a scythe to dig up wet mud – an action that exposes hidden prey such as aquatic insects, crustaceans and small fish. This feeding style is unique to the avocet.

One flew over the Babbler's nest: Pied Cuckoo

Pied Cuckoos are considered harbingers of rain in India. The arrival of the migratory sub-population from Africa (southern India has a resident race) coincides with that of the southwest monsoon winds. But bringing the monsoon to India is not the Pied Cuckoo's only agenda. It is also the time when the Jungle Babbler, the preferred host for this brood parasite, breeds. The cuckoo lays her egg in the babbler's cup-shaped nest, and that is the end of her parental worries. The egg is adapted to mimic the host's egg in colouration, creating the perfect disguise despite its larger size. When the eggs hatch, the larger cuckoo chick demands and consumes far more resources than its step-siblings, often dislodging them from the nest.

A Pied Harrier hunts

It is astonishing how different raptors have adapted to exploit diverse habitats in their own fashion. The dashing Pied Harrier is a grassland and swamp specialist. With wings held in a characteristic 'V', the harrier glides low and parallel to the surface of the tall grass it inhabits. As soon as its razor-sharp eyes detect movement in the grass, the harrier brakes sharply and dives in, emerging moments later with a juicy tidbit. Harriers hunt anything they can catch – large insects, frogs, lizards, snakes, rodents, waterbirds and their chicks are all on the menu. Pied Harriers are winter migrants to India. The male sports a striking black-and-white plumage while the female is chocolate-brown. As they are a serial hunter of field pests, harriers are a boon to farmers.

Parakeet kiss: Plum-headed Parakeets

Plum-headed Parakeets are among the liveliest of Indian birds. Their loud, nasal 'pueenk!' calls never fail to cheer the birdwatcher. Gregarious and always in flocks, parakeets are seed-eaters, and their nutcracking bills are the perfect tools for their diet. Male Plum-headed Parakeets sport cherry-red heads, topped with a purple nape, while females are grey-headed. Plum-headed Parakeets are a common sight in open forests, fields and around monuments, the crevices and cracks of which offer nesting opportunities to these cavity nesters. Pairs are often seen performing endearing courtship displays – a jerky dance followed by a bill-to-bill kiss, accompanied by a lot of singing. A small gift is offered before the female signals acceptance and the pair mates.

Streamside songster: Plumbeous Water-Redstart

Redstarts are characteristically peppy and energetic creatures, and the most winsome among them is the Plumbeous Water-Redstart. A familiar sight in any Himalayan river or hillside stream, the Plumbeous Water-Redstart is called so because of its lead-like colouration. The lead-blue male and the graphite-grey female make an endearing pair.

In a characteristic move, the bird pumps its tail down and fans it, as it enthrals onlookers with its ecstatic high-pitched song that carries over the sound of the water. Despite being chunky in appearance, Plumbeous Water-Redstarts are agile hunters on the wing, frequently performing aerial sallies to catch flying insects. Prey is also caught off the water's surface; the redstart's long claws offer a great grip on pebbles in streams which serve as launchpads. The species nests in holes and crevices in riverside rocks.

Swamp spearman: Purple Heron

The best way to learn that patience is a virtue, is to watch a Purple Heron hunt. The handsome, slender hunter parks itself at the corner of a swamp and freezes into a statue! The heron's strategy is to stand perfectly still and wait until a meal swims within striking range. A fish swims past, and in a fraction of a second, the heron's serpentine neck darts out, shooting its spear-shaped bill right through the body of the fish. The quarry is deftly tossed up and swallowed, again with the characteristic patience of the heron. If you are looking for courses in meditation, I fully recommend grabbing a pair of binoculars and heading to the nearest lake to observe the Purple Heron at work!

Red Crossbills crack the pine code

Coniferous pine seeds lie protected in tough, secure cones and are inaccessible to most animals. But evolution has taught one bizarre passerine to hack the pine's password. The Red Crossbill's bill is unique to its family – the upper mandible curves downward, the lower mandible curves upwards, and both cross each other at the tip! To access the seeds, the crossbill inserts the bill tips into the scales of the pine. In a rare miracle of nature, the jaws open laterally like a pair of forceps, pushing the scales open! The crossbill then deploys its long, sticky tongue to retrieve the seed. Crossbills are also known to exhibit right- or left-handedness – the lower bill can cross the upper to the left or to the right! A truly extraordinary adaptation to double-cross the pine cone!

The male crossbill is red, while females have yellow-green plumage.

Probing the paddyfield: Red-naped Ibis

A familiar sight across India in wetlands, marshes and paddyfields, the Red-naped Ibis is told easily by its characteristic downcurved bill and the bright-red head. The curved bill is a boon not just to the ibis but also to India's farmers.

Crickets, a major agricultural pest, are the ibis' favourite food. When the ibis forages in the fields, it marches slowly, tapping the soft mud with its bill tip, probing for crickets and their larvae. On detecting prey, the bill pierces the mud, digging the critters out. Ibises nest in heronries with gregarious nesters like egrets, herons and cormorants. Although mostly silent, they can be heard 'braying' when they gather at an evening roost.

A jack of all trades: Red-vented Bulbul

One of our most successful and widespread species, the Red-vented Bulbul has one quality that ensures that it makes the most of every ecosystem it inhabits: adaptability. Although it has a slight preference for fruit, it is not choosy. Bulbuls readily exploit every food opportunity, be it fruit or meat, pursuing prey ranging from minute insects and worms to small lizards, while at the same time playing a role in pollination and seed dispersal for a variety of plants and trees. An all-rounder, it is as much at home in the dry scrub habitat as it is in rainforest fringes, across altitudes. Recent range expansions suggest that the species benefits from human-made changes to previously untouched habitats. Red-vented Bulbuls are among the most familiar garden and backyard birds throughout India. Their cup-shaped nests in bushes are among the most common nests a birder comes across.

Ouch, I broke a wing: Red-wattled Lapwing

Red-wattled Lapwings nest on the ground, laying eggs that are mottled and blotched, for better camouflage. But saving your clutch from a predator with keen senses and wily intent, like the Grey Mongoose, takes more than just camouflage: it requires some improvised deception! To begin with, lapwings are among India's noisiest and most relentless birds. They mob and chase anything even remotely perceived as a threat – that includes not just mongooses but also birdwatchers – screeching their typical 'did-hee-doo-it' screams. When mobbing and screeching fail to deter a predator, a final trick is deployed. The parent extends its wing and perches on the ground, feigning an injury. A grown bird in the jaw is better than a few tiny eggs in the bush, right? Wrong! Once the mongoose forsakes the eggs to make a meal of the seemingly injured bird, the lapwing, after ensuring that the predator has moved away from the eggs, takes off!

Red-wattled Lapwings are a common sight in fields, grasslands, marshes, waterbodies and even cities.

Gifting right: River Tern

An agile fisher, the River Tern scans the water for prey, twisting his long, angular wings and forked tail to make swift dives, and picks a fish just off the surface. But today's catch is not meant for the table. It is a gift for his mate! Unlike the human gift of a red rose, this one is of practical value as it happens to be his mate's favourite fish too. A hard-earned catch is a sure way to lure the females in the nesting colony. After marital vows are exchanged and pair bonds formed, he feeds the female before mating with her. Now that is how a true gentleman gifts in style!

River terns are threatened by habitat loss, and face population declines countrywide.

Pink murmuration: Rosy Starlings

You may have watched whirling swarms of tens of thousands of starlings from Europe on viral Internet videos, with your jaws dropping in sheer wonder. The Rosy Starling, a gorgeous pink-and-black winter visitor to India, is among the birds that perform those spectacular aerial manoeuvres in swarms numbering thousands – a phenomenon called 'murmuration'. The starlings form a single mass, flying, twisting and turning in perfect synchrony, holding the onlooker spellbound. A lot happens during this aerial pirouette, which usually takes place just before heading to the evening roost: greetings are offered, information about food sources is exchanged, and safety is assured from predators like falcons and sparrowhawks. The murmuration takes place when the starlings are on their way to their nesting grounds in Central Asia. This journey coincides with the blooming of their favourite flower, the Red Silk Cotton, and they can be seen crowding the flowering trees for nectar.

Turning over a new pebble: Ruddy Turnstone

Run, turn, eat, run, repeat! If you have watched this animated wader, the Ruddy Turnstone, at work, it is easy to guess how it got that name. As the waves recede, the turnstone dashes to the shore, flicking stones over with its bill to expose hiding crustaceans, such as crabs and snails, that are instantly picked and swallowed whole. As the waves advance, the bird runs back, before returning to its task over and over again as each wave recedes. This, however, is only one of the ways in which the turnstone hunts. It also probes the sand using its bill like other waders, digging holes to expose prey, often hammering the shells of snails open by pecking at them. This versatile and energetic wader visits the Indian coasts in winter, flying in from the northern latitudes.

Cackling opportunist: Rufous Treepie

Treepies are somewhat unlikely crows. Sporting a lovely rufous body and a long, graceful grey tail, the Rufous Treepie is unabashedly loud, cackling and chanting a metallic 'konk dank'! A familiar sight across jungles as well as urban gardens, Rufous Treepies are bold opportunists that do not shy away from exploiting any food resource. They change their diet with availability, taking figs and other fruits when in season, while also hunting lizards, bird eggs and nestlings, scorpions, rodents and small snakes, feeding on carrion and even picking ectoparasites from the bodies of deer and antelope (like Sambar and Nilgai). The bird can often be seen digging into a deer's ears and nostrils! Treepies associate with other species such as drongos and babblers in mixed-species feeding flocks.

Foe-turned-friend: Rufous Woodpecker

That ants are a woodpecker's favourite prey is common knowledge. The Rufous Woodpecker specifically prefers Crematogaster or acrobat ants. These stinging ants live in colonies that nest in pagoda-shaped arboreal nests. Well-equipped for defence against ant attacks, the Rufous Woodpecker frequently raids these structures, pecking at the hard exterior of the nest and sucking out the larvae. But what happens when this woodpecker breeds is utterly bizarre and inexplicable, for a unique symbiosis develops between the acrobat ants and their predator. The woodpecker excavates a cavity in the ants' nest, laying its eggs inside! While a few ants and larvae are destroyed in the process, the hosts overlook this. As rent for housing and protection for its chicks, the woodpecker defends the ant nest from other predators, even refraining from eating any inmates of the host nest. Science still does not have an explanation for this strange relationship between predator and prey!

A Rufous-bellied Woodpecker indulges its sweet tongue

The Rufous-bellied Woodpecker is a woodpecker alright, but with a slight twist. While other woodpeckers drill holes in trees for insects and their larvae, this ornate Himalayan resident of oak forests does so for the sap of trees. Often, the woodpecker's prolificity is on full display with a tree of its interest riddled with holes along its trunk! The 'sap wells' that this species drills also attract other birds with a similar palate, such as sibias, nuthatches, barwings, sunbirds and tits, making it a crucial link in the oak forest ecosystem!

Rufous-bellied Woodpeckers are Asia's only sap-feeding woodpecker species.

Ballet in the grass: Sarus Cranes

The most endearing courtship dance of the subcontinent comes from one of its most elegant birds. The Sarus isn't just the world's tallest flying bird, but also an accomplished ballet dancer. The chivalrous male Sarus Crane initiates a duet by holding his wings out and inviting his partner to join, emitting a loud, trumpeting call that resonates across the grassland. Once the female joins, a remarkable performance of song and dance ensues. Necks are twirled, wings spread out and graceful, courteous hops are made in the air as the lovers greet each other with harmonious honks. The birds mate for life and are revered as a symbol of marital fidelity in India. The state bird of Uttar Pradesh, the Sarus inhabits grasslands and paddyfields, and is threatened by habitat loss.

Satyr in love: Satyr Tragopan

As if his rich blood-red plumage was not attractive enough, the male Satyr Tragopan is bestowed with an incredible pattern of contrasting white-on-black spots all over his body, making him a true spectacle. But it is only when he puts on a full-fledged show of his hidden secrets for a potential mate do we learn why he was named after the horned Greek mythical spirit. As the mating dance begins, the crimson 'horns' are unfurled, followed by an extension of the 'Satyr's ears': two bright-blue fleshy extensions at the back of the crown. An elaborately designed gular pouch is distended, revealing the lavish red and blue patterns on it. Then with the wings spread out and the body held erect, the cock sprints after the hen, who appears to enjoy the chase. Once the lovers mate, it is upto the female to raise her brood. Perhaps this is why she ensures every effort is put into winning her heart!

Extremely secretive and rare, these tragopans are seldom seen but their baby-like wailing calls can be heard in the evergreen Himalayan bamboo forests they inhabit.

A Scaly-breasted Munia gathers nesting material

The gregarious and playful Scaly-breasted Munia is encountered most often in grasslands and shrubs, where it gathers in flocks to feed on seeds and berries. In the monsoon when the munia breeds, a visual spectacle unfolds. Scaly-breasted Munias make dome-shaped nests, weaving long grasses and leaves together. For this they must collect blades of grasses several times longer than themselves. As the munias break these blades of green grass and transport them to the nesting site, they appear like birds with green streamers from a distance!

Scaly-breasted Munias, like other species of munias, are heavily sought after for the pet trade.

A hunter improvises: Shikra

The Shikra, one of the commonest raptors in the subcontinent, especially in urban areas, is a bird hunter. But adapting to urban environments demands versatility, and versatility is this successful raptor's forte. Although usually diurnal, Shikras do not mind pushing 'work hours' to dusk, when bats emerge from their roosts in the ledges of old buildings. Well-equipped to ambush birds much faster than bats, the hawk makes a few quick hits before the sun sets completely, usually swallowing the little bats whole. If an evening shift yields more pay for less work, then why not extend the day?

Snake-hunt in the scrubs: Short-toed Snake Eagle

The broad round head of a Short-toed Snake Eagle makes it look more like an owl than an eagle. This raptor prefers scrubs, arid and open country, where it hunts its favourite prey – snakes. Much like the Osprey, this eagle hovers on its broad, rectangular wings, keeping its head perfectly still and its eyes firmly positioned on its target as it calculates the precise moment to dive. As the serpent slithers within striking range, the eagle drops, surrendering its bulk to gravity, only to ascend with lunch in its talons. Hunting with the sun behind it offers the eagle a great advantage as it makes it difficult for prey to detect its approach. The Short-toed Snake Eagle often consumes its prey on the wing, making it seem as though it is enjoying an in-flight spaghetti meal!

A Spot-billed Pelican gulps

Pelicans are well-known for bearing large pouches beneath their bills. The pouch and the muscles of the pelican's tongue are extremely flexible, creating a large basket for catching fish. Spot-billed Pelicans fish in shallow water. Unlike most pelicans that fish in huge flocks, Spot-billed Pelicans seek out their prey alone or in small groups. Swimming at the surface, they scoop up the fish with their bills, using the hook on the upper bill tip to grasp the catch while the pouch attached to the lower bill scoops up the prey along with some water. When the bird swallows the catch, the pouch contracts, pushing the water out of its mouth. Here's one creature that does not mind having a double-chin!

Spot-billed Pelicans can be seen nesting in large colonies – one of the most famous ones is at at Kokkarebellur village in Karnataka.

A Spot-breasted Fantail hunts

Endemic to central and southern India, the Spot-breasted Fantail is a striking bird. Although primarily associated with forests, it is a common backyard and garden bird in most parts. A very active and energetic bird, it is a gifted vocalist that announces its presence unabashedly with a fluty, sing-song whistle. A fantail hunts in the air like a flycatcher, making swift and sharp manoeuvres in pursuit of its winged prey. What truly amazes the onlooker though is its frequent habit of spreading its tail out in a beautiful fan shape. The white tips to the black fan-shaped tail make for a cheerful sight! Fantails make cup-shaped nests in bushes.

Spirit of the mountain stream: Spotted Forktail

If you've ever taken a drink break at a waterfall on a Himalayan forest hike, you must have had the good fortune of meeting the delightfully patterned black-and-white Spotted Forktail. A shy, elegant and animated bird of the hill forests, the Spotted Forktail keeps close to moving water, be it waterfalls or fast-flowing streams. Uttering a metallic screech, it flies into the scene, often bobbing its tail up and down like a wagtail as it moves. Forktails hunt aquatic insects that may be picked off the surface or underwater. Its long feet and claws offer a steady grip on rocks and pebbles, which are the preferred perches from which to dart at the prey. When hunting in shallow waters, its long legs also help keep the body safe above the chilly water of the hillside stream. Forktails nest in holes along the banks of streams.

Dead branch flying: Sri Lanka Frogmouth

A Sri Lanka Frogmouth's idea of spending the day is to sleep, pretending to be a dead leaf or twig. If startled, the frogmouth slowly extends its neck, appearing to be a dried extension of the branch it is perched on! While the female sports a dry-leaf orange plumage, the male is grey-brown, both mottled generously for enhanced crypsis. At dusk, the nocturnal pair starts to call, emitting guttural screeches and squawks, before setting off to hawk insects in the air. Built like falcons, their long wings and tails make them agile fliers and aerial hunters. The frogmouth is called so because of its exceptionally wide gape, which is used to snap at large flying insects like moths. As dawn sets in, the night hunters re-transform into grumpy twigs and leaves, returning to their preferred perch and resuming their favourite daytime activity: slumber.

A White-browed Bushchat struts in the scrubs

A bird of deserts and scrub land, the White-browed or Stoliczka's Bushchat is known for a peculiar dance move, aptly termed the 'puff-and-roll' display. An insectivore, it spends most of its time on the ground where it forages, and it is on the ground that this strange performance is enacted. The bird puffs its feathers up, assuming a ball-like shape, rolling its body from side to side rhythmically until the back is entirely erect! The purpose of this dance is yet to be ascertained by science. Courtship is a bleak possibility because both sexes perform the dance, often in the absence of a mate. Scientists speculate that the dance is either a territorial display or aids the bird when feeding. Or could the bird be simply humming a tune to itself in its mind as it puffs and rolls? Or infusing the arid landscape with some light-hearted mischief that only birds are capable of?

Mud apartments: Streak-throated Swallows

Streak-throated or Indian Cliff Swallows congregate along the banks of waterbodies during the breeding season, not for a drink but to collect wet mud. The birds dig the soil with their tiny bills, rolling the clay into little balls that are carried in their mouths to the nesting site. Laying these balls one atop another, they laboriously construct a funnel-shaped nest with an opening in the centre. The particles of the mud are cemented together using the bird's saliva. Hundreds of such nests made of dried clay can be seen at a nesting colony, with those at the centre being the most secure ones. The best spots in the colony are earned with experience and time, while the fringes usually go to newbies. Streak-throated Swallow nesting colonies are frequently encountered along bridges and embankments. One of the best places to witness this at close quarters is on a boat ride in the Ranganathittu Bird Sanctuary in Karnataka.

A Tawny-breasted Wren Babbler skulks

If you're a birdwatcher who has tried to track this bird, I am sure that, like me, you too would be convinced that the word 'skulker' may have been invented specially for a Wren Babbler. Spending its entire day in dense thickets covering foothills, it rarely ever makes an appearance. What makes matters worse (for birders and the Wren Babbler's predators) is that it is marked cryptically and blends in expertly with the foliage. The only trait that belies its ultra-reclusive life is its cheerful whistle, which the bird indulges in when marking its territory or courting a mate, making it a creature that's far easier to hear than to spot.

The Tawny-breasted Wren Babbler is endemic to Meghalaya's Khasi Hills.

A cliffhanger: Wallcreeper

Coveted by birdwatchers, Wallcreepers are at home where only the best rock climbers dare to venture – steep rocky hillsides and cliffs in the Himalayas. This astonishing species is often encountered on drives in the mountains, where roads cut through steep cliffs. The Wallcreeper may sport a dull grey-black exterior, but reveals its true colours when it opens its wings. You are left spellbound as it splashes open its striking crimson wings that contrast with the bold white edges to its tail. The Wallcreeper periodically flicks its wings open and shut, offering tantalizing glimpses of its brilliant colouration for the awestruck birder trying to keep up. The bird's thin, long bill is the perfect tool for its lifestyle as it hunts spiders, insects and their larvae within the cracks and crevices of cliffs.

Wallcreepers make their nests from moss and vegetation in the safety of crevices along cliff slopes and are extremely territorial. In the winter, these birds migrate to the sub-Himalayan region where they can be seen on boulder stream beds or even on retention walls of dams and canals.

Panic in the marshes: Western Marsh Harrier

It is a calm winter morning at a lake where huge flocks of several species of migratory dabbling ducks – that have flown in from great distances – have gathered to feed. Suddenly, out of nowhere, there is utter chaos in the air; the flocks make helter-skelter dashes in different directions, completely disrupting the serenity of the moment! The source of the chaos is a migratory raptor – the Western Marsh Harrier. A rich gold- and chocolate-coloured female prowls the lake with her wings held in a 'V' shape typical of harriers, flying low and parallel to the surface of the water. Singling out a duck in a flock is a challenge. Once the target has been isolated, the killer swoops, grabbing the duck in her talons and carrying it away. As she watches over her hunting ground, shredding her breakfast into pieces, the calmness of the morning is slowly restored, only to be disrupted by her next hunt.

Venom for breakfast: White-bellied Sea Eagle

The bold, contrasting stripes on the Striped Sea Snake's body are a visual warning: it is one of the most venomous snakes in the world. Most predators pay heed to this warning, keeping a safe distance, but not the White-bellied Sea Eagle. Although the eagle hunts a wide range of prey from fish to waterbirds, sea snakes are a favourite. Sea snakes do not possess gills and must swim to the surface frequently to catch a breath. Timing its dive precisely, the eagle strikes down in a fraction of a second and bags the catch that has just appeared on the sea's surface. As the sea snake tries to inflict a bite mid-air, the eagle must manoeuvre and realign its grip before it reaches its perch, where the aggressive snake is swiftly beheaded using the massive hook on the bird's bill.

Sea snakes are frequently hunted when White-bellied Sea Eagles have eaglets to feed.

Leap of faith: White-winged Wood Ducks

Unlike ground-nesting ducks, White-winged Wood Ducks nest in tree cavities, often several feet from the ground. While this guarantees safety from terrestrial predators, it is only temporary respite, as the ducklings must follow their mother to the nearest waterbody to feed within a few days of hatching. Nagging with her quacks, the mother encourages the chicks to leave the safety of the nest and jump to the ground. Her pleas, coupled with their hunger, are enough to persuade the chicks. One by one they make the leap, the leaf-littered forest floor acting as a cushion for their soft bodies. The ducklings follow the mother on their very first swim, forming a train behind her.

The White-winged Wood Duck is the state bird of Assam. Very secretive and shy, it is rarely encountered and is endangered because of hunting and habitat loss.

Flautist fig-eaters: Yellow-footed Green Pigeons

The first rays of the sun smile upon the deciduous canopy in a central Indian forest, and with it come large flocks of Yellow-footed Green Pigeons. Their rich green colour comes from carotenoid pigments in their diet of fruits. Gregarious and always moving around in flocks, green pigeons love to bask in the early hours of the morning before they start foraging. Greeting each other (as well as birdwatchers) with an accentuated fluty yodel, there is never a dull moment around a Yellow-footed Green Pigeon flock! Green pigeons are compulsive fruit eaters and love to feast on figs. They are among the fig's most important dispersers. The species is the state bird of Maharashtra, where it is known as 'Hariyal'.

A good listener: Yellow-crowned Woodpecker

Woodpeckers are renowned for pecking at trees and hunting insects. But an overlooked quality, of being good listeners, is what makes them such efficient hunters. As the Yellow-crowned Woodpecker prepares to hunt, it rests its ear against the bark of a tree, seeking the sounds of insects and larvae moving inside. Once the prey is tracked, the head-banging begins. The chisel-bill is hammered with terrific speed as chips of dead wood fly past, boring a hole into the trunk. The woodpecker's tongue is a miraculous organ. It is so long that it is stored rolled around the skull inside the bird's head! This acts as a shock-absorber for the brain when hammering a tree. The tongue, equipped with barbs in the tip for foolproof grasping of the prey, is inserted into the hole to pull out juicy tidbits. Yellow-crowned Woodpeckers, like the rest of the family, excavate nest cavities in trees to raise their young. The species was christened 'Mahratta Woodpecker', after the state of Maharashtra where it was first described from. The name probably also refers to the colours that the male woodpecker sports on his head, which resembles the bright turbans of Maratha warriors!

Wave-walker: Wilson's Storm-Petrel

Being pelagic birds, Wilson's Storm-Petrels are so light that all they need to do to stay aloft is hold their wings high up, even when there is not much of a breeze. They are called so because once upon a time sailors thought them to be divine warnings of impending storms. Wilson's Storm-Petrels are among the world's most abundant birds. They feed on krill and plankton in a manner unique to their family. The birds always feed in large groups, hovering over the water surface and dipping their feet a few times. This behaviour, called 'foot-pattering', tends to attract plankton and krill to the surface, which are promptly caught in the tube-shaped bill. Storm-petrels are also known to follow ships to feast on discarded scraps. Weighing only 40 g, the Wilson's Storm-Petrel is the smallest warm-blooded animal to breed in Antarctica! In India, it is seen only in the coastal waters, several kilometres away from the shore.

High-octane hunt: Shaheen Falcon

The majestic Shaheen Falcon, a resident race of the fastest living creature, the Peregrine Falcon, lives in rocky cliffs and hills adjoining forests. These perches act as perfect vantage points to launch attacks on its choice of prey – birds such as swifts and Rock Pigeons. When the target is spotted and locked, the Shaheen takes position and transforms into a missile, launching into its famed 390-kmph dive. Such is the impact of this dive that a mere touch of the talon is enough to take the life of the hapless pigeon! The quarry is quickly retrieved and taken to a rocky perch to be devoured.

The Shaheen's superior hunting abilities are celebrated vividly in Urdu and Persian literature, especially in the works of Allama Iqbal.

Glossary

Arboreal	Living in trees
Arthropod	A group of invertebrates having a segmented body and exoskeleton
Carotenoids	Yellow, orange and red colour pigments that are produced by plants as well as by some organisms including bacteria, fungi and algae
Caudal	Refers to the tail or the hind part of the body
Crustaceans	A group of arthropods that includes crabs, lobsters, shrimp and other shellfish
Crypsis	The ability of an animal to hide from a predator using camouflage
Echolocation	The means of locating objects and animals through reflected sound
Ectoparasites	Organisms that live on the skin or outer covering of a host and may be harmful
Epiphytes	Plants that grow on other plants
Gape	In birds, refers to the interior of the open mouth
Gastropods	A class of molluscs that includes animals such as snails, slugs and abalones
Hypoxia	A condition of low oxygen levels in the body
Ineluctable	Inescapable
Keratinized	Covered with a layer of hard protein that forms over hair and nails
Montane	Mountainous
Nictitating	Some animals have a transparent or translucent third eyelid called the nictitating membrane. It helps protect the eye from injury.
Opposable Talons	In some raptors, one toe can move forward or back so that it can have two facing forward and two facing backward for a better grip on prey.
Polygamous	In a polygamous relationship, one or both spouses have multiple partners
Polygynous	A male that has more than one mate is called polygynous
Precocial	Refers to young animals that are independent at birth, and can move around and find food
Preen glands	These are organs that produce an oily substance that birds coat their feathers with

Index

Bibliography

Birkhead, Tim (2013): *Bird Sense*. Bloomsbury, US.

Rasmussen, Pamela C. & John C. Anderton (2012): *Birds of South Asia: The Ripley Guide. Volume 2: Attributes and Status*. Second edition. Smithsonian Institution and Lynx Edicions, US.

Kazmierczak, Krys (2006): *A Field Guide to the Birds of India, Sri Lanka, Pakistan, Nepal, Bhutan, Bangladesh and the Maldives*. Om Book Service, New Delhi.

Naoroji, Rishad (2008): *Birds of Prey of the Indian Subcontinent*. Om Book Service, New Delhi.

Ranga, Madhur Mohan, Vijay Kumar Koli & Chhaya Bhatnagar (2011): 'Resettlement and nesting of Streak-throated swallow Hirundo fluvicola Blyth 1855'. Retrieved from https://www.researchgate. net/publication/230700859_Resettlement_and_nesting_of_Streak-throated_swallow_Hirundo_ fluvicola_Blyth_1855.

Raman, T.R. Shankar (2017): 'Why the evolutionary link between flowerpeckers and mistletoes is crucial to the forests'. Retrieved from https://scroll.in/magazine/846313/under-the-mistletoe-how-alittle-birds-love-for-a-parasitic-plant-could-save-the-worlds-forests.

Jones, Benji (2018): 'Meet the Woodpecker that impersonates a Snake'. Retrieved from https://www.nationalgeographic.com/animals/2018/09/woodpecker-wryneck-impersonate-mimic-snake-animals/

Raman, T.R. Shankar (2009): 'Welcome back, Warblers'. Retrieved from https://www.thehindu.com/features/magazine/Welcome-back-warblers/article16889743.ece

Tyler, Stephanie J. & Stephen Ormerod (2010): *The Dippers. Poyser Monographs*. Academic Press, UK.

Agnihotri, Samira (2015): 'What's that Racket: Of drongos and acoustic landscapes'. Retrieved from http://jlrexplore.com/explore/from-the-field/racket-tailed-drongo

Banerjee, Ananda (2016): 'The Chilgoza's last stand'. Retrieved from https://www.livemint.com/Sundayapp/LL7EYm8GxYdn76klm0eVSJ/The-Chilgozas-last-stand.html

Amoghavarsha, J.S. (2013): *River Terns of Bhadra*. Directed by Amoghavarsha J.S.

BBC (2007): *Planet Earth Series*. Documentary. Produced by BBC, UK.

Acknowledgements

I owe my gratitude and a session of allopreening to a number of people for making this book happen:

My late mother Sulabha, for her free spirit, courage, and her infectious and immortal enthusiasm. My ex-wife Rithika for her reviews, critique, and for her indispensable company on innumerable birding trips. My brother Rohit for guiding me each time I got stuck, for sharing an obsessive love for birds and cinema with me, and for keeping me on my toes by competing with me over 'life-lists'! My father Ashit for being an unwavering pillar of support and for being my (unenthusiastic) daily balcony-birding companion over coffee. Kripa for her acute artistic eye that helps me elevate my art and my vision of the world around me. Dr Tarique and Swati Sani for taking me on my first bird walk, and for being a constant source of motivation and encouragement. T.R. Shankar Raman, ecologist and writer with the Nature Conservation Foundation, for agreeing to pen the foreword for the book, and for some of the most insightful and enjoyable nature writing from India in modern times (the Nilgiri Flowerpecker sequence is inspired by his splendid article on flowerpeckers). Ornithologists Bikram Grewal, Umesh Srinivasan, Samira Agnihotri and Raman Kumar for their invaluable inputs on bird behaviour. Friends and family who helped me with their support and backing each time I needed it through the course of this book – Tina Fernandes, Pritha Dey, Dipsha Kriplani, Dhwani Chandel, Prerna Bindra, Munmun Dhalaria, Sejal Mehta and Bijal Vachharajani. To birding companions without whose help and company I would not have seen several species illustrated in this book: Abhishek Gulshan, Divya Mudappa, Binanda Hathiboruah, Madhu Behera, Phurpa Atjepu, Ranjan Kumar Das, Deborshee Gogoi, Ramit Singal, Karthikeyan Srinivasan, Tenzin Ragbye, Deepa Mohan, Tharangini Bala, Drama Mekola, Rohit Jha and Rekha Warrier. To my mentors Bittu Sahgal, Radhika Suri, Rupa Gandhi Chowdhry, Nandini Velho and Millo Tasser for their support. To the Juggernaut Team – Anita Mani, Nishtha Kapil, Chiki Sarkar and Ajith Kumar. To the BNHS team, Dr Deepak Apte, Vibhuti Dedhia and Maithreyi M.R. To team Siyahi – Mita Kapur and Urvi Bhuwania. To the artists whose work and styles have been prime sources of inspiration for the book: my imaginary mentor Genndy Tartakosvky (*Dexter's Laboratory* and *Samurai Jack*), Charlie Harper and Sanjay Patel. To my canine friends and family: Naughty, Laxman, Keeto, Fifi, Mahabir, Jenny, Uday, Doginder Singh, Srishti, Sakshi, Chandni and WallE, for helping me appreciate ethology better. To Nibbles, a Red-vented Bulbul chick I was raising, who could not make it to adulthood, but gave me some much-needed tuitions on bird behaviour.

To birds, right from the rare and elusive Bugun Liocichlas of Arunachal to the House Sparrows nesting in my bird boxes, for inculcating mischief, romance and humour in an otherwise grumpy old man!

A Note on the Author

ROHAN CHAKRAVARTY is a cartoonist and illustrator, and the creator of *Green Humour*, a series of cartoons on wildlife and conservation. *Green Humour* is the first series of comics from India to be distributed internationally by a major syndicate. His work has won awards from UNDP, Sanctuary Asia, WWF International and the Royal Bank of Scotland. His books include three *Green Humour* compilations, *Naturalist Ruddy* and *The Great Indian Nature Trail with Chunmun*. Rohan takes his birding quite seriously despite not being taken very seriously by birds themselves! He is notorious for rolling up into a ball like a pangolin to avoid answering the phone or meeting people.

Website: http://www.greenhumour.com/

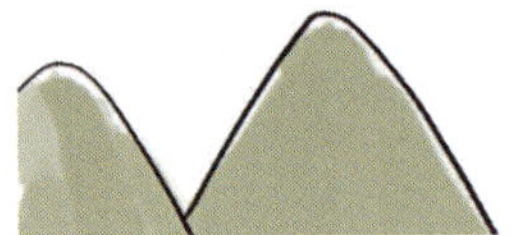

About Indian Pitta

Indian Pitta is India's first dedicated book imprint for bird and nature lovers, conservationists and policymakers. Our books about wildlife and natural history go beyond field/identification guides, to explore the bigger mosaic of habitats, ecosystems and human interactions that touch the lives of birds and animals. Successful conservation programmes, troubling environmental challenges, personal exploration of a landscape, deep dives into the ecology of a species, the quest for a rare species and the sheer joy of birding – these are some of the ideas that you can expect to explore within the pages of our books.

Also Available

ISBN: 978-93-5345-181-3
Price: ₹499/-

ISBN: 978-93-5345-164-6
Price: ₹1,299/-

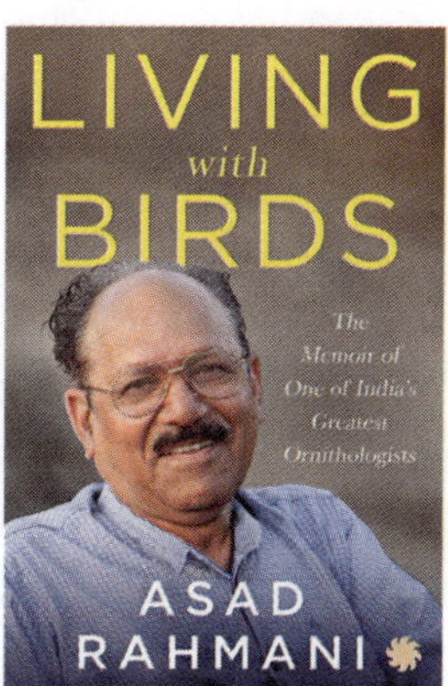

ISBN: 978-93-5345-415-9
Price: ₹599/-

ISBN: 978-93-5345-320-6
Price: ₹499/-